WILD NIGHTS

Heart Wisdom from Five Women Poets

Foreword by Lisa Locascio
Illustrated by Claire Whitmore

ixia
PRESS

Mineola, New York

Bibliographical Note

Wild Nights: Heart Wisdom from Five Women Poets is a new work,
first published by Ixia Press in 2018.

International Standard Book Number

ISBN-13: 978-0-486-82426-0
ISBN-10: 0-486-82426-8

IXIA PRESS
An imprint of Dover Publications, Inc.

Manufactured in the United States by LSC Communications
82426801   2018
www.doverpublications.com/ixiapress

CONTENTS

AMY LOWELL

SARA TEASDALE

EDNA ST. VINCENT MILLAY

FOREWORD

In the Azure Spaces

For a while there, we heard a lot of popular variants of the word *feel*. First came "the feels" and then the phrase "that feel when," quickly shortened to the hashtaggable "TFW." Although those professing feels were not exclusively young women, this was the demographic identified as the feels' primary arbiter, witches-initiate in that interstitial realm of desire and pain. There, the girls generated emotion so powerful that it took independent form, what Tibetan Buddhists and, much later, the movie director David Lynch called a *tulpa*—an internal sensation so pervasive it becomes its own being, its own world. From their realm's dizzying heights, these feelers rained down judgments on those who provoked them.

Since then we have held in our cultural dreaming a dialectic of feels, a way of knowing through feel. Pop stars are popular feel-triggers—and baby animals and politicians and unexpected workaday heroics against hatred and injustice. The feel is both coveted—nothing can be sold or bought without it—and feared, cast often as fickle, pernicious, and infantile. Not accidentally, the feel is always gendered female. Women and their emotions: for those who seek to control the former, the latter always presents a problem. Smile. Don't make a scene. And never, ever write down your feels, especially not in what Sharon Olds calls a "language of blood like praise all over the body" in her poem "The Language of the Brag."

> I have done what you wanted to do,
>   Walt Whitman,
> Allen Ginsberg, I have done this thing,
>
> I and the other women this exceptional
> act with the exceptional heroic body,
> this giving birth, this glistening verb,
> and I am putting my proud American boast
> right here with the others.

Olds incanted this fierce proclamation in the 1970s, her explicit topic literal childbirth. Fertility, creativity, and reproduction are bodied experiences, but they require language in order to be conveyed—recorded and valorized and bemoaned and celebrated and, yes, bragged about. That the gendered feminine voice on the page has both been celebrated and condemned for its attentions to the tandem proprioception of spirit and heart is a statement of its unique and enduring power. Thus, the little volume you hold in your hands is nothing less than a grimoire, a spell book ancient and magicked, political by virtue of its existence, heartrending in the extreme. A thing to be wise of, to explore, to dissect and revere its gleaming parts.

Among our most ancient fragments of poetry is the work of a woman, Sappho, about whom little is known but much is felt—a legacy she commanded into existence through her verse. "From my swift blood that went and came/A thousand little shafts of flame," the poet from Lesbos wrote (Alfred Lord Tennyson translation), spelling her lush imagination into being and into perpetuity. Sappho's capacity for evoking the intricacies of erotic passion and longing feels contemporary, as does her fearless habit of naming and renaming desire, or as she warily terms the experience, "Love once more, the limb-dissolving King" (J. Addington Symonds translation). For her, poetry comes from the numinous divine—the "azure spaces" ("The Muses," John Myers O'Hara translation). Aphrodite travels in her "cerulean car" ("To The Goddess of Love," Herbert translation) to intervene and assist with the feel-wars waged by us mortals.

Emily Dickinson, in contrast, lived in a past much more familiar to us than Sappho's, but her solitary nature and aura of cultivated mystery imbued her poetry with a weird American mood that continues to draw us in and put us off. Reading Dickinson, one travels an embodied and inscribed landscape riven with memory and experience. "On the strangest sea" of the self, Dickinson is reckless and vivid in her pursuit of ecstatic reverie, unshy about claiming ownership of her lived experiences. "He touched me, so I live to know," she proclaims, "I the dart revere." That dart—simultaneously the heat-seeking missile of romantic craving and the penetrating instinct of her peerless eye—beckons the reader inside, where anything can happen.

Next to Emily Dickinson and Sappho, Amy Lowell and Sara Teasdale are considerably less famous, which makes their discovery that much more delicious for the contemporary seeker of feels high and fine. There is no poem quite like Lowell's "Fireworks," a phantasmagoria of shade, shape, and action that purports to describe a type of hatred, an emotionally intense bond, we glean by the end, that the word barely begins to apprehend.

And when you meet me, you rend asunder
And go up in a flaming wonder
Of saffron cubes, and crimson moons,
And wheels all amaranths and maroons.

Golden lozenges and spades
Arrows of malachites and jades,
Patens of copper, azure sheaves.
As you mount, you flash in the glossy leaves.

The tender erotic longing of "A Rainy Night" alone can make
the concerns of one evening in the early twentieth century
seem quite near at hand indeed—a hand already singed in
"Opal," wherein Lowell pines, "The touch of you burns
my hands like snow." Reading Lowell can be a bit like being
inside her poem "The Letter." The reader, tossed between
torrential, craving, insistent imagery like "Heart's blood
for your drinking" ("Absence") and "white heart-flame of
polished silver" ("Madonna of the Evening Flowers") might
themselves muse, "And I scald alone, here under the fire/Of
the great moon."

If Lowell is that great moon—the tarot card often signifying
both the unconscious and fierce emotion, the occult and the
turning-inward of passionate conviction—then Teasdale can
rightly be identified as her companion in the Major Arcana:
the High Priestess. Pain and pleasure swirl at the Priestess's
feet as she considers the delights and disappointments of
the world with impassive wisdom, her keening spirit hidden
deep beneath magisterial robes. "My heart like the bird in the
tree/is calling, calling, calling," Teasdale writes in "Twilight,"

sending that self out to spread itself against every crevice of the fairyland of feeling. "I am the pool of blue / that worships the vivid sky . . . I am the pool of gold/when sunset burns and dies" ("Peace"). Hers is a voice without vanity or illusion, equally plain in its pronouncements of passion and mortality, knowingly awaiting the day "all my joyous body/puts off the red and white" ("The Answer"). Such knowledge is the task of the poet, a mantle she wears upon her priestess throne: "I caught life back against my breast/and kissed it, scars and all" ("Wood Song").

The final poet in this volume, Edna St. Vincent Millay, is also a woman of individual conviction. She yearns, but with a world-weary sense that love, like the month of April and spring itself, is oft an "an idiot, babbling and strewing flowers" ("Spring"). The beloved "Witch-Wife" of the eponymous poem is that much more magical because the poem's speaker recognizes "she will never be all mine." That's the thing about the feels; as soon as you think you have a handle on them, they have a way of snaking out of your grasp and becoming something else entirely. "Suffer me to cherish you," St. Vincent Millay commands in "Mariposa," in keeping with the honest depictions of love offered by this collection: as often suffering as cherishing, as much angst as beauty.

Because that's where the power lies: in this conversation between old and new, present and past, in the interstices between the sensations we know are only our own and the dignifying loveliness of discovering that other people have felt this way too. More than brag, spell, lament, or song, writing at its root is the attestation of existence, the singular statement of the real. "Summer sang in me," St. Vincent

Millay testifies in "Sonnet XLIII," a fact of which you hold the proof in your hands.

If women are "feelmancers," and poetry is, as we all know, another word for magic, try this secret rite. Read a poem three times. Let your eyes unfocus on the gentle page. Trace with them the lighted paths through time and space, the connections and calls and answers that close the gap between then and now. Close your eyes and tell me what you see, who you feel.

In "After Parting," Teasdale reaches through millennia to touch Sappho:

> I set my shadow in his sight
> and I have winged it with desire,
> That it may be a cloud by day,
> And in the night a shaft of fire.

You can do it too. Notch that arrow, dipped in the pure stuff—want, desire, love, passion, the white heart-flame, the cerulean car of the goddesses. Point it to the firmament. Let it fly.

Lisa Locascio
Visiting Assistant Professor of Creative Writing
Wesleyan University
February 2018

WILD
NIGHTS

SAPPHO

Come, Venus, come
Hither with thy golden cup,
Where nectar-floated flowerets swim.

Fill, fill the goblet up;
These laughing lips shall kiss the brim—
Come, Venus, come!

—Anonymous

To the Goddess of Love

Venus, daughter of the mighty Jove,
Most knowing in the mystery of love,
Help me, oh help me, quickly send relief,
And suffer not my heart to break with grief.

If ever thou didst hear me when I prayed,
Come now, my goddess, to thy Sappho's aid.
Orisons used, such favour hast thou shewn,
From heaven's golden mansions called thee down.

See, see, she comes in her cerulean car,
Passing the middle regions of the air.
Mark how her nimble sparrows stretch the wing,
And with uncommon speed their Mistress bring.

Arrived, and sparrows loosed, hastens to me;
Then smiling asks, What is it troubles thee?
Why am I called? Tell me what Sappho wants.
Oh, know you not the cause of all my plaints?

I love, I burn, and only love require;
And nothing less can quench the raging fire.
What youth, what raving lover shall I gain?
Where is the captive that should wear my chain?

Alas, poor Sappho, who is this ingrate
Provokes thee so, for love returning hate?
Does he now fly thee? He shall soon return;
Pursue thee, and with equal ardour burn.

Would he no presents at thy hands receive?
He will repent it, and more largely give.
The force of love no longer can withstand;
He must be fond, wholly at thy command.

When wilt thou work this change? Now, Venus, free,
Now ease my mind of so much misery;
In this amour my powerful aider be;
Make Phaon love, but let him love like me.

—translated by Herbert

The Muses

Hither now, O Muses, leaving the golden
House of God unseen in the azure spaces,
Come and breathe on bosom and brow and kindle
    Song like the sunglow;

Come and lift my shaken soul to the sacred
Shadow cast by Helicon's rustling forests;
Sweep on wings of flame from the middle ether,
    Seize and uplift me;

Thrill my heart that throbs with unwonted fervor,
Chasten mouth and throat with immortal kisses,
Till I yield on maddening heights the very
    Breath of my body.

—translated by John Myers O'Hara

Fragment 16

Some say that the fairest thing
upon the dark earth is a host of horsemen,
and some say a host of foot soldiers,
and others again a fleet of ships,
but for me it is my beloved.

—translated by J. M. Edmonds

To a Woman

That man seems to me peer of gods,
who sits in thy presence, and hears close to him
thy sweet speech and lovely laughter,
that indeed makes my heart flutter in my bosom.

For when I see thee but a little,
I have no utterance left, my tongue is broken down,
and straightway a subtle fire has run under my skin;
with my eyes I have no sight, my ears ring,
sweat pours down, and a trembling seizes all my body;
I am paler than grass, and seem in my
madness little better than one dead.
But I must dare all, since one so poor....

—translated by H. T. Wharton

The moon hath left the sky,
Lost is the Pleiads' light;
    It is midnight
    And time slips by;
But on my couch alone I lie.

—translated by J. Addington Symonds

Beauty

I

Like the sweet apple which reddens upon the
    topmost bough,
A-top on the topmost twig—which the pluckers
    forgot, somehow—
Forgot it not, nay, but got it not, for none
    could get it till now.

II

Like the wild hyacinth flower which on the
    hills is found,
Which the passing feet of the shepherds for
    ever tear and wound,
Until the purple blossom is trodden into the
    ground.

—translated by Dante Gabriel Rossetti

I

Peer of the gods, the happiest man I seem
Sitting before thee, rapt at thy sight, hearing
Thy soft laughter and they voice most gentle,
    Speaking so sweetly.

II

Then in my bosom my heart wildly flutters,
And, when on thee I gaze never so little,
Bereft am I of all power of utterance,
    My tongue is useless.

III

There rushes at once through my flesh tingling fire,
My eyes are deprived of all power of vision,
My ears hear nothing by sounds of winds roaring,
    And all is blackness.

IV

Down courses in streams the sweat of emotion,
A dread trembling o'erwhelms me, paler than I
Than dried grass in autumn, and in my madness
    Dead I seem almost.

—translated by Edwin M. Cox

Fragment 40

Ah, love is bitter and sweet,
but which is more sweet,
the sweetness
or the bitterness?
none has spoken it.

Love is bitter,
but can salt taint sea-flowers,
grief, happiness?

Is it bitter to give back
love to your lover
if he crave it?

Is it bitter to give back
love to your lover
if he wish it
for a new favorite?
who can say,
or is it sweet?

Is it sweet
to possess utterly?
or is it bitter,
bitter as ash?

—interpreted by H.D.

Fatima

Last night, when some one spoke his name,
From my swift blood that went and came
A thousand little shafts of flame
Were shiver'd in my narrow frame.

—translated by Alfred Lord Tennyson

Long Ago

Long ago beloved, thy memory, Atthis,
Saddens still my heart as the soft Æolic
Twilight deepens down on the sea, and fitful
    Winds that have wandered

Over groves of myrtle at Amathonte
Waft forgotten passion on breaths of perfume.
Long ago, how madly I loved thee, Atthis!
    Faithless, light-hearted

Loved one, mine no more, who lovest another
More than me; the silent flute and the faded
Garlands haunt the heart of me thou forgettest,
    Long since thy lover.

—translated by John Myers O'Hara

Fragments

This will I now sing deftly to please my girlfriends.

To you, fair maids, my mind changes not.

Stand face to face, friend . . . and unveil the grace
   in thine eyes.

                              —translated by H. T. Wharton

According to my weeping:
it and all care let buffeting winds
bear away.

—translated by H. T. Wharton

Now Eros shakes my soul,
a wind on the mountain falling on the oaks.

—translated by H. T. Wharton

The stars about the fair moon
in their turn hide their bright
face when she at about her full
lights up all earth with silver.

—translated by H. T. Wharton

Summer

Slumber streams from quivering leaves that listless
Bask in heat and stillness of Lesbian summer;
Breathless swoons the air with the apple-blossoms'
    Delicate odor;

From the shade of branches that droop and cover
Shallow trenches winding about the orchard,
Restful comes, and cool to the sense, the flowing
    Murmur of water.

—translated by John Myers O'Hara

What country maiden charms thee,
However fair her face,
Who knows not how to gather
Her dress with artless grace?

—translated by H. T. Wharton

But place those garlands on thy lovely hair,
Twining the tender sprouts of anise green
With skilful hand; for offerings and flowers
Are pleasing to the Gods, who hate all those
Who come before them with uncrowned heads.

—translated by C. D. Yonge

Lo, Love once more, the limb-dissolving King,
The bitter-sweet impracticable thing,
Wild-beast-like rends me with fierce quivering.

—translated by J. Addington Symonds

Kupris

[Come] to me from Crete to this holy dwelling,
where your lovely grove
of apple trees is, and your altars smoking
    with frankincense

herein cold water rushes through the apple branches,
and the entire space is overshadowed by roses,
and from the shimmering leaves
    sleep pours down.

Here a horse-nourishing meadow blooms
with spring flowers, and the winds
blow gentle

In this place, you, Kupris, taking up garlands
pour nectar gracefully
in golden cups and mix it
    with our festivities.

—translated by Gregory Nagy and Casey Dué

EMILY

DICKINSON

Pain has an element of blank;
It cannot recollect
When it began, or if there were
A day when it was not.

It has no future but itself,
Its infinite realms contain
Its past, enlightened to perceive
New periods of pain.

The brain within its groove
Runs evenly and true;
But let a splinter swerve,
'Twere easier for you'
To put the water back
When floods have slit the hills,
And scooped a turnpike for themselves,
And blotted out the mills!

I've got an arrow here;
    Loving the hand that sent it,
I the dart revere.

Fell, they will say, in "skirmish"!
    Vanquished, my soul will know,
By but a simple arrow
    Sped by an archer's bow.

I hide myself within my flower,
That wearing on your breast,
You, unsuspecting, wear me too—
And angels know the rest.

I hide myself within my flower,
That, fading from your vase,
You, unsuspecting, feel for me
Almost a loneliness.

You left me, sweet, two legacies—
A legacy of love
A Heavenly Father would content,
Had He the offer of;

You left me boundaries of pain
Capacious as the sea,
Between eternity and time,
Your consciousness and me.

Hope is the thing with feathers
That perches in the soul,
And sings the tune without the words,
And never stops at all,

And sweetest in the gale is heard;
And sore must be the storm
That could abash the little bird
That kept so many warm.

I've heard it in the chillest land
And on the strangest sea;
Yet never, in extremity,
It asked a crumb of me.

Our share of night to bear,
Our share of morning,
Our blank in bliss to fill,
Our blank in scorning.

Here a star, and there a star,
Some lose their way.
Here a mist, and there a mist,
Afterwards—day!

I had no time to hate, because
The grave would hinder me,
And life was not so ample I
Could finish enmity.

Nor had I time to love; but since
Some industry must be,
The little toil of love, I thought,
Was large enough for me.

My river runs to thee:
Blue sea, wilt welcome me?

My river waits reply.
Oh, sea, look graciously!

I'll fetch thee brooks
From spotted nooks—

Say, sea,
Take me!

Wild nights! Wild nights!
Were I with thee,
Wild nights should be
Our luxury!

Futile the winds
To a heart in port,—
Done with the compass,
Done with the chart.

Rowing in Eden!
Ah! The sea!
Might I but moor
To-night in thee!

Come slowly, Eden!
Lips unused to thee,
Bashful, sip thy jasmines,
As the fainting bee,

Reaching late his flower,
Round her chamber hums,
Counts his nectars—enters,
And is lost in balms!

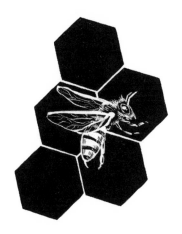

He touched me, so I live to know
That such a day, permitted so,
    I groped upon his breast.
It was a boundless place to me,
And silenced, as the awful sea
    Puts minor streams to rest.

And now, I'm different than before,
As if I breathed a superior air,
    Or brushed a royal gown;
My feet, too, that had wandered so,
My gypsy face transfigured now
    To tenderer renown.

I have no life but this,
To lead it here;
Nor any death, but lest
Dispelled from there;

Nor ties to earths to come,
Nor action new,
Except through this extent,
The realm of you.

Heart, we will forget him!
　　You and I, to-night!
You may forget the warmth he gave,
　　I will forget the light.

When you have done, pray tell me,
　　That I my thoughts may dim;
Haste! lest while you're lagging,
　　I may remember him!

To lose thee, sweeter than to gain
    All other hearts I knew.
'Tis true the drought is destitute,
    But then I had the dew!

The Caspian has its realms of sand,
    Its other realms of sea;
Without the sterile perquisite
    No Caspian could be.

Proud of my broken heart since thou didst
   break it,
Proud of the pain I did not feel till thee,
Proud of my night since thou with moons
   doth slake it,
Not to partake thy passion, my humility.

The Face we choose to miss,
Be it but for a day—
As absent as a hundred years
When it has rode away.

Beauty crowds me till I die,
Beauty, mercy have on me!
But if I expire today,
Let it be in sight of thee.

For each ecstatic instant
We must an anguish pay
In keen and quivering ratio
To the ecstasy.

For each beloved hour
Sharp pittances of years,
Bitter contested farthings
And coffers heaped with tears.

We outgrow love like other things
And put it in the drawer,
Till it an antique fashion shows
Like costumes grandsires wore.

If I can stop one heart from breaking,
I shall not live in vain;
If I can ease one life the aching,
Or cool one pain,
Or help one fainting robin
Unto his nest again,
I shall not live in vain.

AMY

LOWELL

Fireworks

You hate me and I hate you,
And we are so polite, we too!

But whenever I see you I burst apart
And scatter the sky with my blazing heart.
It spits and sparkles in stars and balls,
Buds into roses, and flares and falls.

Scarlet buttons, and pale green disks,
Silver spirals and asterisks,
Shoot and tremble in a mist
Peppered with mauve and amethyst.

I shine in the window and light up the trees,
And all because I hate you, if you please.

And when you meet me, you rend asunder
And go up in a flaming wonder
Of saffron cubes, and crimson moons,
And wheels all amaranths and maroons.

Golden lozenges and spades,
Arrows of malachites and jades,
Patens of copper, azure sheaves.
As you mount you flash in the glossy leaves.

Such fireworks as we make, we two!
Because you hate me and I hate you.

The Bungler

You glow in my heart
Like the flames of uncounted candles.
But when I go to warm my hands,
My clumsiness overturns the light,
And then I stumble
Against the tables and chairs.

The Tree of Scarlet Berries

The rain gullies the garden paths
And tinkles on the broad sides of grass blades.
A tree, at the end of my arm, is hazy with mist.
Even so, I can see that it has red berries,
A scarlet fruit,
Filmed over with moisture.
It seems as though the rain,
Dripping from it,
Should be tinged with colour.
I desire the berries.
But, in the mist, I only scratch my hand on the thorns.
Probably, too, they are bitter.

Anticipation

I have been temperate always,
But I am like to be very drunk
With your coming.
There have been times
I feared to walk down the street
Lest I should reel with the wine of you,
And jerk against my neighbors
As they go by.
I am parched now, and my tongue is horrible in my
   mouth,
But my brain is noisy
With the clash and gurgle of filling wine-cups.

The Letter

Little cramped words scrawling all over the paper
Like draggled fly's legs,
What can you tell of the flaring moon
Through the oak leaves?
Or of my uncertain window and the bare floor
Spattered with moonlight?
Your silly quirks and twists have nothing in them
Of blossoming hawthorns,
And this paper is dull, crisp, smooth, virgin of
   loveliness
Beneath my hand.

I am tired, Beloved, of chafing my heart against
The want of you;
Of squeezing it into little inkdrops,
And posting it.
And I scald alone, here, under the fire
Of the great moon.

A Year Passes

Beyond the porcelain fence of the pleasure-garden,
I hear the frogs in the blue-green ricefields;
But the sword-shaped moon
Has cut my heart in two.

Obligation

Hold your apron wide
That I may pour my gifts into it,
So that scarcely shall your two arms hinder them
From falling to the ground
I would pour them upon you
And cover you,
For greatly do I feel this need
Of giving you something,
Even these poor things.

Dearest of my Heart!

Opal

You are ice and fire,
The touch of you burns my hands like snow.
You are cold and flame.
You are the crimson of amaryllis,
The silver of moon-touched magnolias.
When I am with you,
My heart is a frozen pond
Gleaming with agitated torches.

A Rainy Night

Shadows,
And white, moving light,
And the snap and sparkle of rain on the window,
An electric lamp in the street
Is swinging, tossing,
Making the rain-runnelled window-glass
Glitter and palpitate.
In its silver lustre
I can see the old four-post bed,
With the fringes and balls of its canopy.
You are lying beside me, waiting,
But I do not turn.
I am counting the folds of the canopy.
You are lying beside me, waiting,
But I do not turn.
In the silver light you would be too beautiful,
And there are ten pleats on this side of the bed
    canopy,
And ten on the other.

Madonna of the Evening Flowers

All day long I have been working,
Now I am tired.
I call: "Where are you?"
But there is only the oak tree rustling in the wind.
The house is very quiet,
The sun shines in on your books,

On your scissors and thimble just put down,
But you are not there.
Suddenly I am lonely.
Where are you?
I go about searching.

Then I see you,
Standing under a spire of pale blue larkspur,
With a basket of roses on your arm.
You are cool, like silver,
And you smile.
I think the Canterbury bells are playing little tunes,

You tell me that the peonies need spraying,
That the columbines have overrun all bounds,

That the pyrus japonica should be cut back and
  rounded.
You tell me these things.
But I look at you, heart of silver,
White heart-flame of polished silver,
Burning beneath the blue steeples of the larkspur,
And I long to kneel instantly at your feet,
While all about us peal the loud,
sweet *Te Deums* of the Canterbury bells.

A Decade

When you came, you were like red wine and honey,
And the taste of you burnt my mouth with its
   sweetness.
Now you are like morning bread—
Smooth and pleasant.
I hardly taste you at all for I know your savour,
But I am completely nourished.

The Taxi

When I go away from you
The world beats dead
Like a slackened drum.
I call out for you against the jutted stars
And shout into the ridges of the wind.
Streets coming fast,
One after the other,
Wedge you away from me,
And the lamps of the city prick my eyes
So that I can no longer see your face.
Why should I leave you,
To wound myself upon the sharp edges of the night?

The Giver of Stars

Hold your soul open for my welcoming.
Let the quiet of your spirit bathe me
With its clear and rippled coolness,
That, loose-limbed and weary, I find rest,
Outstretched upon your peace, as on a bed of ivory.

Let the flickering flame of your soul play all about me,
That into my limbs may come the keenness of fire,
The life and joy of tongues of flame,
And, going out from you, tightly strung and in tune,
I may rouse the blear-eyed world,
And pour into it the beauty which you have begotten.

Absence

My cup is empty to-night,
Cold and dry are its sides,
Chilled by the wind from the open window.
Empty and void, it sparkles white in the moonlight.
The room is filled with the strange scent
Of wisteria blossoms.
They sway in the moon's radiance
And tap against the wall.
But the cup of my heart is still,
And cold, and empty.

When you come, it brims
Red and trembling with blood,
Heart's blood for your drinking;
To fill your mouth with love
And the bitter-sweet taste of a soul.

Aubade

As I would free the white almond from the green husk
So would I strip your trappings off,
Beloved.
And fingering the smooth and polished kernel
I should see that in my hands glittered a gem beyond
counting.

Prime

Your voice is like bells over roofs at dawn
When a bird flies
And the sky changes to a fresher color.

Speak, speak, Beloved.
Say little things
For my ears to catch
And run with them to my heart.

A Gift

See! I give myself to you, Beloved!
My words are little jars
For you to take and put upon a shelf.
Their shapes are quaint and beautiful,
And they have many pleasant colours and lustres
To recommend them.
Also the scent from them fills the room
With sweetness of flowers and crushed grasses.

When I shall have given you the last one,
You will have the whole of me,
But I shall be dead.

A Petition

I pray to be the tool which to your hand
Long use has shaped and moulded till it be
Apt for your need, and, unconsideringly,
You take it for its service. I demand
To be forgotten in the woven strand
Which grows the multi-coloured tapestry
Of your bright life, and through its tissues lie
A hidden, strong, sustaining, grey-toned band.
I wish to dwell around your daylight dreams.
The railing to the stairway of the clouds.
To guard your steps securely up, where streams
A faery moonshine washing pale the crowds
Of pointed stars. Remember not whereby
You mount, protected, to the far-flung sky.

Miscast II

My heart is like a deft pomegranate
Bleeding crimson seeds
And dripping them on the ground.
My heart gapes because it is ripe and over-full,
And its seeds are bursting from it.

But how is this other than a torment to me!
I, who am shut up, with broken crockery,
In a dark closet!

Autumn

They brought me a quilled, yellow dahlia,
Opulent, flaunting.
Round gold
Flung out of a pale green stalk.
Round, ripe gold
Of maturity,
Meticulously frilled and flaming,
A fire-ball of proclamation:
Fecundity decked in staring yellow
For all the world to see.
They brought a quilled, yellow dahlia,
To me who am barren
Shall I send it to you,
You who have taken with you
All I once possessed?

SARA

TEASDALE

Twilight

Dreamily over the roofs
    The cold spring rain is falling;
Out in the lonely tree
    A bird is calling, calling.

Slowly over the earth
    The wings of night are falling;
My heart like the bird in the tree
    Is calling, calling, calling.

Night Song at Amalfi

I asked the heaven of stars
What I should give my love—
It answered me with silence,
Silence above.

I asked the darkened sea
Down where the fishers go—
It answered me with silence,
Silence below.

Oh, I could give him weeping,
Or I could give him song—
But how can I give silence,
My whole life long?

Off Algiers

Oh give me neither love nor tears,
    Nor dreams that sear the night with fire,
Go lightly on your pilgrimage
    Unburdened by desire.

Forget me for a month, a year,
    But, oh, beloved, think of me
When unexpected beauty burns
    Like sudden sunlight on the sea.

The Look

Strephon kissed me in the spring
    Robin in the fall,
But Colin only looked at me
    And never kissed at all.

Strephon's kiss was lost in jest,
    Robin's lost in play,
But the kiss in Colin's eyes
    Haunts me night and day.

But Not to Me

The April night is still and sweet
    With flowers on every tree;
Peace comes to them on quiet feet,
    But not to me.

My peace is hidden in his breast
    Where I shall never be;
Love comes to-night to all the rest,
    But not to me.

Faults

They came to tell your faults to me,
They named them one by one;
I laughed aloud when they were done,
I knew them all so well before,—
Oh, they were blind, too blind to see
Your faults had made me love you more.

After Parting

Oh, I have sown my love so wide
    That he will find it everywhere;
It will awake him in the night,
    It will enfold him in the air.

I set my shadow in his sight
    And I have winged it with desire,
That it may be a cloud by day,
    And in the night a shaft of fire.

Tides

Love in my heart was a fresh tide flowing
Where the starlike sea gulls soar;
The sun was keen and the foam was blowing
High on the rocky shore.

But now in the dusk the tide is turning,
Lower the sea gulls soar,
And the waves that rose in resistless yearning
Are broken forevermore.

After Love

There is no magic any more,
    We meet as other people do,
You work no miracle for me
    Nor I for you.

You were the wind and I the sea—
    There is no splendor anymore,
I have grown listless as the pool
    Beside the shore.

But though the pool is safe from storm
    And from the tide has found surcease,
It grows more bitter than the shore,
    For all is peace.

New Love and Old

In my heart the old love
    Struggled with the new;
It was ghostly waking
    All night through.

Dear things, kind things,
    That my old love said,
Ranged themselves reproachfully
    Round my bed.

But I could not heed them,
    For I seemed to see
The eyes of my new love
    Fixed on me.

Old love, old love
    How can I be true?
Shall I be faithless to myself
    Or to you?

The Kiss

I hoped that he would love me,
    And he has kissed my mouth,
But I am like a stricken bird
    And cannot reach the south.

For though I know he loves me,
    Tonight my heart is sad;
His kiss was not so wonderful
    As all the dreams I had.

Gifts

I gave my first love laughter,
    I gave my second tears,
I gave my third love silence
    Through all the years.

My first love gave me singing,
    My second eyes to see,
But oh, it was my third love
    Who gave my soul to me.

November

The world is tired, the year is old,
    The fading leaves are glad to die,
The wind goes shivering with cold
    Among the rushes dry.

Our love is dying like the grass,
    And we who kissed grow coldly kind,
Half glad to see our old love pass
    Like leaves along the wind.

Wisdom

When I have ceased to break my wings
Against the faultiness of things,
And learned that compromises wait
Behind each hardly opened gate,
When I can look Life in the eyes,
Grown calm and coldly wise,
Life will have given me the Truth,
And taken in exchange—my youth.

Wood Song

I heard a wood thrush in the dusk
Twirl three notes and make a star—
My heart that walked with bitterness
Came back from very far.

Three shining notes were all he had,
And yet they made a starry call—
I caught life back against my breast
And kissed it, scars and all.

Come

Come, when the pale moon like a petal
    Floats in the pearly dusk of spring,
Come with arms outstretched to take me,
    Come with lips pursed up to cling.

Come, for life is a frail moth flying,
    Caught in the web of the years that pass,
And soon we two, so warm and eager,
    Will be as the grey stones in the grass.

Love-Free

I am free of love as a bird flying south in the autumn,
Swift and intent, asking no joy from another,
Glad to forget all of the passion of April
    Ere it was love-free.

I am free of love, and I listen to music lightly,
But if he returned, if he should look at me deeply,
I should awake, I should awake and remember
    I am my lover's.

A Prayer

Until I lose my soul and lie
  Blind to the beauty of the earth,
Deaf though a lyric wind goes by,
  Dumb in a storm of mirth;

Until my heart is quenched at length,
And I have left the land of men
Oh let me love with all my strength
  Careless if I am loved again.

Peace

Peace flows into me
 As to the tide to the pool by the shore;
 It is mine forevermore,
It ebbs not back like the sea.

I am the pool of blue
 That worships the vivid sky;
 My hopes were heaven-high,
They are all fulfilled in you.

I am the pool of gold
 When sunset burns and dies—
 You are my deepening skies,
Give me your stars to hold.

The Answer

When I go back to earth
And all my joyous body
Puts off the red and white
That once had been so proud,
If men should pass above
With false and feeble pity,
My dust will find a voice
To answer them aloud:

"Be still, I am content,
Take back your poor compassion,
Joy was a flame in me
Too steady to destroy;
Lithe as a bending reed
Loving the storm that sways her—
I found more joy in sorrow
Than you could find in joy."

The Coin

Into my heart's treasury
I slipped a coin
That time cannot take
Nor a thief purloin,—
Oh better than the minting
Of a gold-crowned king
Is the safe-kept memory
Of a lovely thing.

EDNA

ST. VINCENT MILLAY

First Fig

My candle burns at both ends;
    It will not last the night;
But ah, my foes, and oh, my friends—
    It gives a lovely light!

Midnight Oil

Cut if you will, with sleep's dull knife,
Each day to half its length, my friend,—
The years that time takes off *my* life,
    He'll take from off the other end!

The Merry Maid

Oh, I am grown so free from care
    Since my heart broke!
I set my throat against the air,
    I laugh at simple folk!

There's little kind and little fair
    Is worth its weight in smoke
To me, that's grown so free from care
    Since my heart broke!

Lass, if to sleep you would repair
    As peaceful as you woke,
Best not besiege your lover there
    For just the words he spoke
To me, that's grown so free from care
    Since my heart broke!

Afternoon on a Hill

I will be the gladdest thing
    Under the sun!
I will touch a hundred flowers
    And not pick one.

I will look at cliffs and clouds
    With quiet eyes,
Watch the wind bow down the grass,
    And the grass rise.

And when lights begin to show
    Up from the town,
I will mark which must be mine,
    And then start down!

Songs of Shattering

I

The first rose on my rose-tree
    Budded, bloomed, and shattered,
During sad days when to me
    Nothing mattered.

Grief of grief has drained me clean;
    Still it seems a pity
No one saw,—it must have been
    Very pretty.

Ashes of Life

Love has gone and left me and the days are all alike;
    Eat I must, and sleep I will,—and would that night
    were here!
But ah!—to lie awake and hear the slow hours strike!
    Would that it were day again!—with twilight near!

Love has gone and left me and I don't know what to do;
    This or that or what you will is all the same to me;
But all the things that I begin I leave before I'm
    through,—
    There's little use in anything as far as I can see.

Love has gone and left me,—and the neighbors knock
  and borrow,
    And life goes on forever like the gnawing of a
    mouse,—
And to-morrow and to-morrow and to-morrow and
    to-morrow
    There's this little street and this little house.

Sorrow

Sorrow like a ceaseless rain
    Beats upon my heart.
People twist and scream in pain,—
Dawn will find them still again;
This has neither wax nor wane,
    Neither stop nor start.

People dress and go to town;
    I sit in my chair.
All my thoughts are slow and brown;
Standing up or sitting down
Little matters, or what gown
    Or what shoes I wear.

Witch-Wife

She is neither pink nor pale,
    And she never will be all mine;
She learned her hands in a fairy-tale,
    And her mouth on a valentine.

She has more hair than she needs;
    In the sun 'tis a woe to me!
And her voice is a string of colored beads,
    Or steps leading into the sea.

She loves me all that she can,
    And her ways to my ways resign;
But she was not made for any man,
    And she never will be all mine.

Thursday

And if I loved you Wednesday,
    Well, what is that to you?
I do not love you Thursday—
    So much is true.

And why you come complaining
    Is more than I can see.
I loved you Wednesday,—yes—but what
    Is that to me?

To the Not Impossible Him

How shall I know, unless I go
    To Cairo and Cathay,
Whether or not this blessed spot
    Is blest in every way?

Now it may be, the flower for me
    Is beneath my nose;
How shall I tell, unless I smell
    The Carthaginian rose?

The fabric of my faithful love
    No power shall dim or ravel
Whilst I stay here,—but oh, my dear,
    If I should ever travel!

V

If I should learn, in some quite casual way,
That you were gone, not to return again—
Read from the back-page of a paper, say,
Held by a neighbor in a subway train,
How at the corner of this avenue
And such a street (so are the papers filled)
A hurrying man—who happened to be you—
At noon to-day had happened to be killed,
I should not cry aloud—I could not cry
Aloud, or wring my hands in such a place—
I should but watch the station lights rush by
With a more careful interest on my face,
Or raise my eyes and read with greater care
Where to store furs and how to treat the hair.

The Philosopher

And what are you that, wanting you,
    I should be kept awake
As many nights as there are days
    With weeping for your sake?

And what are you that, missing you,
    As many days as crawl
I should be listening to the wind
    And looking at the wall?

I know a man that's a braver man,
    And twenty men as kind,
And what are you, that you should be
    The one man on my mind?

Yet women's ways are witless ways,
    As any sage will tell,—
And what am I, that I should love
    So wisely and so well?

Sonnet III

Oh, think not I am faithful to a vow!
Faithless am I save to love's self alone.
Were you not lovely I would leave you now;
After the feet of beauty fly my own.
Were you not still my hunger's rarest food,
And water even to my wildest thirst,
I would desert you—think not but I would!—
And seek another as I sought you first.
But you are mobile as the veering air,
And all your charms more changeful than the tide,
Whether to be inconstant is no care:
I have but to continue at your side.
So wanton, light and false, my love, are you,
I am most faithless when I am most true.

Sonnet IV

I shall forget you presently, my dear,
So make the most of this, your little day,
Your little month, your little half a year,
Ere I forget, or die, or move away,
And we are done forever; by and by
I shall forget you, as I said, but now,
If you entreat me with your loveliest lie
I will protest you with my favorite vow.
I would indeed that love were longer-lived,
And vows were not so brittle as they are,
But so it is, and nature has contrived
To struggle on without a break thus far,—
Whether or not we find what we are seeking
Is idle, biologically speaking.

Eel-Grass

No matter what I say,
    All that I really love
Is the rain that flattens on the bay,
    And the eel-grass in the cove;
The jingle-shells that lie and bleach
    At the tide-line, and the trace
Of higher tides along the beach:
    Nothing in this place.

Spring

To what purpose, April, do you return again?
Beauty is not enough.
You can no longer quiet me with the redness
Of little leaves opening stickily.
I know what I know.
The sun is hot on my neck as I observe
The spikes of the crocus.
The smell of the earth is good.
It is apparent that there is no death.
But what does that signify?
Not only under the ground are the brains of men
Eaten by maggots.
Life in itself
Is nothing,
An empty cup, a flight of uncarpeted stairs.
It is not enough that yearly, down this hill,
April
Comes like an idiot, babbling and strewing flowers.

Mariposa

Butterflies are white and blue
In this field we wander through.
Suffer me to take your hand.
Death comes in a day or two.

All the things we ever knew
Will be ashes in that hour:
Mark the transient butterfly,
How he hangs upon the flower.

Suffer me to take your hand.
Suffer me to cherish you
Till the dawn is in the sky.
Whether I be false or true,
Death comes in a day or two.

Ebb

I know what my heart is like
      Since your love died:
It is like a hollow ledge
Holding a little pool
      Left there by the tide,
      A little tepid pool,
Drying inward from the edge.

Sonnet XLIII

What lips my lips have kissed, and where, and why,
I have forgotten, and what arms have lain
Under my head til morning; but the rain
Is full of ghosts tonight, that tap and sigh
Upon the glass and listen for reply,
And in my heart there stirs a quiet pain
For unremembered lads that not again
Will turn to me at midnight with a cry.
Thus in the winter stands the lonely tree,
Nor knows what birds have vanished one by one,
Yet knows its boughs more silent than before:
I cannot say what loves have come and gone,
I only know that summer sang in me
A little while, that in me sings no more.

The Dream

Love, if I weep it will not matter,
    And if you laugh I shall not care;
Foolish am I to think about it,
    But it is good to feel you there.

Love, in my sleep I dreamed of waking,—
    White and awful the moonlight reached
Over the floor, and somewhere, somewhere,
    There was a shutter loose,—it screeched!

Swung in the wind,—and no wind blowing!—
    I was afraid, and turned to you,
Put out my hand to you for comfort,—
    And you were gone! Cold, cold as dew,

Under my hand the moonlight lay!
    Love, if you laugh I shall not care,
But if I weep it will not matter,—
    Ah, it is good to feel you there!

Passer Mortuus Est

Death devours all lovely things:
    Lesbia with her sparrow
Shares the darkness,—presently
    Every bed is narrow.

Unremembered as old rain
    Dries the sheer libation;
And the little petulant hand
    Is an annotation.

After all, my erstwhile dear,
    My no longer cherished,
Need we say it was not love,
    Now that love is perished?

BIOGRAPHIES

Sappho

For being perhaps the world's most famous female poet, shockingly little is known of Sappho's life and only slightly more remains of her poetry. We can assume that Sappho was born around 630 BC to 610 BC—over 2,600 years ago—on the Greek isle of Lesbos. Her work was cataloged in the Library of Alexandria, lauded by Plato, mentioned by Herodotus, and considered the equal of Homer. But today's fragments show only a partial glimpse at its scope. Of an estimated ten thousand lines of poetry, only a handful of mostly complete poems and a few even smaller hundred fragments remain. It is possible that the early church disapproved of her work and discouraged its copying, but even as the existing work available to us has dwindled, the legend and draw of Sappho's work has remained.

The poems included in this anthology are all drawn from interpretations and translations of the extant fragments and poems accessible to us. They showcase how radically Sappho's work infiltrated the canon of English-language poetry as well as how radically different interpretations of her voice can be. Many of these versions were compiled by Henry Thornton Wharton, who published *Sappho: Memoir, Text, Selected Renderings and a Literal Translation* in 1887 to collect the original Greek and its various renditions in English. She was a strong influence on the poets Algernon Charles Swinburne, Lord Byron,

Elizabeth Barrett Browning, T. S. Eliot, Ezra Pound, H.D., and many others, all of whom interpreted her in the light of their own poetic voice. More recently, Anne Carson and Jeanette Winterson have stripped away some of the embellishments that have accrued over time to present her work in as unadorned a state as possible. While we will probably never be able to piece back together the full body of Sappho's work or even its place in the society and literature of its time, her status as a wellspring of inspiration for generations of poets, writers, and creators is untouchable.

She has long been known for her erotic subject matter and style, though each era approaches her writing from a different angle. Whether or not she was a lesbian, she has long been associated with homoeroticism, and the other poets included in this collection were uniformly inspired by her example as a path-breaking female author.

Emily Dickinson

Emily Dickinson created her monumental life's body of work of almost 1,800 poems from her family home. Born in Amherst, Massachusetts, in 1830, where she died in 1886, she enrolled briefly at Mount Holyoke after finishing preparatory school. But her life thereafter saw her slowly retreat into her own private world, establishing a reputation as an eccentric spinster. While she maintained many active correspondences with friends, including with several men who have been rumored as potential love interests (as was her sister-in-law Susan Gilbert), her in-person contacts with the world outside of her own family were few. Whether despite or because of this, her poetry ranged far and wide across every subject imaginable, often drawing on mortality and religion, but straying into the topic of love as well. Virtually unpublished until after her death, when her sister Lavinia brought her work to light, Dickinson's unique and penetrating voice and off-kilter sensibility slowly made her one of the premier American poets.

Amy Lowell

Amy Lowell was born into a prominent New England family in 1874. While her family was strongly associated with academic pursuits—her father Augustus Lowell was a president of Harvard and her brother Percival became a renowned astronomer—it was considered inappropriate for Amy to attend college because she was a woman. She took up poetry in 1902 and went on to author several collections. Her poetry was championed by *The Atlantic Monthly*, and during her fifteen-year-long career, she not only expanded her own style but also championed the work of other authors such as Carl Sandburg.

A practitioner of free verse with an interest in imagism, classic Chinese poetry, she freely drew inspiration from the work of others, from Sappho to Ezra Pound and John Keats. She was awarded a posthumous Pulitzer Prize for Poetry for her collection "What's O'Clock." But after her death she was often disparaged for her weight and her lesbian identity, and her name lost the first-rank status and recognition it deserved. An iconoclast known for regularly smoking cigars in public and for her public relationship with actress Ada Dwyer Russell (the subject of many of Lowell's erotic poems), she was a woman well before her time.

Sara Teasdale

Born in St. Louis, Missouri, in 1884, Sara Teasdale became part of a group of young women artists, the Potters, who published their own monthly literary magazine. After her marriage to Ernst Filsinger, Teasdale moved to New York City to pursue her career as a poet. She would win the first Columbia Poetry Prize in 1918 (later renamed the Pulitzer Prize).

The poet Vachel Lindsay wanted to marry Teasdale, but he was rejected. After divorcing her husband in 1929, she rekindled their friendship. But Lindsay killed himself two years before she went on to commit suicide in 1933 at age forty-nine. No longer widely known today, her lyrical, expressive work is still often set to music, whether in choral arrangements or for piano.

Edna St. Vincent Millay

Originally from a small town in Maine, Edna St. Vincent Millay was born in 1892 to parents who would later divorce. In her teen years, she grew up with a single mother who stressed the importance of being independent and self-supporting. Her poem "Renascence" caught the attention of the public when she submitted it in competition and won financial support to enroll in classes at Vassar College at age twenty-one. After graduating in 1917, she moved to Greenwich Village and immediately became a fixture of the literature scene, becoming a published playwright as well as a published poet and cofounding New York City's Cherry Lane Theater.

In 1923, she was the third woman to win the Pulitzer Prize in Poetry and received the Frost Medal for her contributions to American poetry in 1943. Until her death in 1950, she also was politically active, from her antiwar stance during the two World Wars to protests against the Sacco and Vanzetti convictions to her outspoken antifascism. Openly bisexual, she was a nonconformist in every regard, a feminist in an open marriage, as well as a strikingly accomplished writer. Her distinctive voice heralded a new era for women in American life.

INDEX OF FIRST LINES